Love Letters From Papa God

The Lord says, be at peace.
I am with you always.
I _love you_, My daughter!

Cathie McDonald

Love Letters From Papa God

By
Cathie McDonald

Copyright 2024 Cathie McDonald

All rights reserved. This book is protected by the copyright laws of the United States of America. This book may not be copied or reprinted for commercial gain or profit. The use of short quotations or occasional page copying for personal or group study is permitted and encouraged.

The Passion Translation® is a registered trademark of Passion & Fire Ministries, Inc.**123**. The Passion Translation® New Testament with Psalms, Proverbs, and Song of Songs, 2020 Edition is published by BroadStreet Publishing® Group, LLC1. The copyright for The Passion Translation® belongs to Passion & Fire Ministries, Inc.**123**. When quoted, one of the following credit lines must appear on the copyright page of the work: Scripture quotations marked TPT are from The Passion Translation®. Copyright © 2017, 2018, 2020 by Passion & Fire Ministries, Inc. Used by permission. All rights reserved. ThePassionTranslation.com**2**.

LOVINGLY DEDICATED TO:

MY BLESSING OF A HUSBAND, BOB, WHO WAS USED BY GOD TO BRING ME BACK TO LIFE AND TO TEACH ME WHAT TRUE GODLY LOVE IS.

MY INCREDIBLE MOTHER WHO CHOSE THE SCREAMING BABY AT THE FOSTER HOME AND GAVE ME A BEAUTIFUL LIFE AND THE MOST AMAZING DAD WHO EVER LIVED!

Contents

Chapter 1 - How It All Began Pg. 9

Chapter 2 - Love Letters Pg 15

Chapter 3 - Prophetic Words Pg 47

Chapter 4 - A Word From Papa
　　　　God to the Readers Pg 55

Chapter 5 - Salvation Prayer. Pg 71

How It All Began

God is always speaking. Sometimes He speaks through ministers. Sometimes He speaks through music. Sometimes He speaks through His living Word - The Bible. God also gives different gifts to His people to speak into others. There are Pastors, Teachers, Apostles, evangelists, and prophets. Prophets hear directly from Holy Spirit and deliver God's words to God's people. They can deliver these messages in several different ways.

I first discovered that I had prophetic giftings when I was part of a deliverance ministry starting in 2010. I had been working as a transcriptionist or scribe in the medical field for many years. God has gifted me in the natural with a passion for this particular line of work, so as I started my journey with a ministry, it came naturally to be able to write down what the Lord was saying personally to the person that we, as a team, were ministering to. Others in the ministry before me, and after me, also had this gifting. I see it as a form of a prophetic personal word. I like to call them Love Letters. As I read them out to the person it was written for,

I am told that they very often have tears in their eyes, as it touches them personally, and they know that their Papa God truly cares about them. I don't often have the privilege of seeing these emotions while I am reading the letter to them, but I know it is a very healing experience for them.

Sometimes, the letter brings a level of healing itself. God orchestrates the entire session, as others get scriptures or visions that often match what God says in the letter. It is so incredible to see how Papa God pieces it all together.

I wrote this book to be able to share with you the beautiful things that our Papa God is saying to His Children by sharing the actual love letters that the Lord wrote through me during sessions I have served in. Even though they were written for a specific person at the time, they are to be shared with others who can and will receive their own healing. I have not included any names or dates with these letters.

Just like any other prophetic word given, if the letters, or anything in them, speak to you then please receive them as your very own. I pray that these letters bless you and help you to know and feel how very much your Papa God loves you!

2 Peter 1:21 - No true prophesy comes from human initiative but is inspired by the moving of the Holy Spirit upon those who spoke the message that came from God

1 Corinthians 14:3 - But when someone prophesies, he speaks to encourage people, to build them up, and to bring them comfort.

Ephesians 4:11 - And he has appointed some with grace to be apostles, and some with grace to be prophets, and some with grace to be evangelists.

Acts 2:17 - This is what I will do in the last days. I will pour out my Spirit on everybody and cause your sons and daughters to prophesy, and your young men will see visions, and your old men will experience dreams from God. .

Love Letters

MY SWEET DAUGHTER,

I AM HERE. I AM ALWAYS HERE. I HAVE NEVER LEFT YOUR SIDE, AND I PROMISE I NEVER WILL. LEAN ON ME, CLING TO ME, CRY TO ME. I AM YOUR SOLID ROCK. I AM ALL YOU NEED. LET ME TAKE YOUR HAND AND WALK WITH YOU EVERY SINGLE STEP OF THE WAY. I HAVE THE PERFECT PATH FOR YOU. TRUST ME TO WALK WITH YOU ONE STEP AT A TIME. YOU DO NOT NEED TO WORRY ABOUT THE FUTURE. LET US TAKE EVERY DAY AT A TIME - TOGETHER ALWAYS. I AM YOUR BELOVED AND YOU ARE MINE. I LOVE YOU MORE THAN YOU CAN EVEN IMAGINE, MY PRECIOUS GIRL. MY LOVE FOR YOU IS HEALING AND RESTORING. I WANT YOU TO BE WHOLE AGAIN.

LOVE NEVER-ENDING,

YOUR PAPA GOD

MY SWEET SON,

THANK YOU FOR TRUSTING ME WITH YOUR LIFE, YOUR HEALTH, YOUR EVERYTHING. I LOVE YOU WITH AN EVERLASTING LOVE THAT SURROUNDS YOU ON ALL SIDES. I AM YOUR SOURCE AND YOUR STRENGTH. I AM ALL THAT YOU NEED. I HAVE SO MUCH FOR YOU, MY SON. I AM LAYING OUT A PATH BEFORE YOU THAT WILL BRING YOU PEACE, PROVISION, HEALTH, AND WHOLENESS. JUST GRAB A HOLD OF ME AND DO NOT LET GO. I PROMISE THAT I WILL NEVER LET GO OF YOU. I LOVE YOU AND CHERISH YOU TOO MUCH. LET ME FIGHT FOR YOU WHEN YOU FEEL THAT YOU DO NOT HAVE THE STRENGTH. I AM YOUR STRENGTH. I AM YOUR HEALER.

LOVE ALWAYS,

YOUR PAPA GOD

MY BEAUTIFUL DAUGHTER,

YOU ARE:

PRECIOUS TO ME.
CHOSEN BY ME.
MORE COSTLY THAN GOLD.
MORE PRECIOUS THAN DIAMONDS.
MINE ALWAYS.
MY FAVORITE.
ALWAYS WANTED.
NEVER FORSAKEN.
ALWAYS ON MY MIND.
BOUGHT WITH A PRICE.
SURROUNDED WITH LOVE.
SAVED BY GRACE.
CREATED WITH A PURPOSE.

I LOVE YOU MORE THAN WORDS CAN SAY.
YOU MAKE ME SMILE.
I AM ALWAYS WITH YOU, AND I ALWAYS
WILL BE. YOU CAN COUNT ON THAT!

LOVE NEVER-ENDING,

YOUR DADDY GOD
YOUR EVERYTHING
YOUR REDEEMER

I AM REVEALING MYSELF TO YOU, MY DAUGHTER, IN A WAY YOU HAVE NEVER EXPERIENCED BEFORE. MY LOVE FOR YOU IS SURROUNDING YOU LIKE A CONSTANT SHIELD. MY POWER IS FLOWING THROUGH YOU, RENEWING AND RESTORING EVERY CELL, EVERY CONNECTION, RIGHT DOWN TO YOUR VERY DNA. YOU ARE RESTORED, YOU ARE RESET, YOU ARE WHOLE! THIS IS MY WILL FOR YOU, TO BE EXACTLY WHO I CREATED YOU TO BE. GRAB A HOLD OF IT AND DON'T LET GO! DO NOT EVER LET GO, MY BELOVED PRECIOUS DAUGHTER. I NEED YOU IN THE BATTLE. BE STRONG AND COURAGEOUS. STAND STRONG!

I LOVE YOU!

YOUR RESTORER
YOUR CREATOR
YOUR DELIVERER

MY DAUGHTER,

REST IN ME. I AM ALWAYS RIGHT BY YOUR SIDE. I PROMISED TO NEVER LEAVE YOU OR FORSAKE YOU, AND I NEVER WILL. YOU CAN COUNT ON THAT, MY BELOVED GIRL. YOU ARE PRECIOUS TO ME. I SENT MY ONLY SON TO DIE FOR YOU EVEN BEFORE YOU WERE BORN. I HAVE A PLAN FOR YOU. MY PLANS ARE FOR YOUR GOOD. THE ENEMY HAS TRIED TO TAKE YOU OUT, BUT I HAVE PROTECTED YOU AT EVERY TURN. YOU ARE MINE AND I AM YOURS. GIVE IT ALL TO ME, MY DAUGHTER, AND LET ME HEAL YOU, FREE YOU, DELIVER YOU. I WANT YOU FREE IN EVERY AREA OF YOUR LIFE. YOU AND I HAVE SO MUCH TO DO TOGETHER. WALK WITH ME AND WATCH ME MOVE.

I LOVE YOU ALWAYS,

YOUR PAPA GOD
YOUR EVERYTHING

MY PRECIOUS CHILD,

OH, HOW BEAUTIFUL YOU ARE TO ME, INSIDE AND OUT. YOU RADIATE MY LOVE. THANK YOU FOR BEING MY LIGHT AND MY EXAMPLE ON THIS EARTH. YOU ARE A SURRENDERED VESSEL, AND TOGETHER WE CAN DO GREAT AND MIGHTY THINGS. THE ENEMY HAS TRIED TO BEAT YOU DOWN, BUT I AM HOLDING YOU UP WITH MY MIGHTY HANDS. I WILL NOT LET YOU FALL. I AM YOUR SOURCE AND YOUR STRENGTH. I AM ALL THAT YOU NEED, MY CHILD. LET ME WHISPER TO YOU ALL THE PLANS THAT I HAVE FOR YOU TO BRING YOU GOOD, TO BATHE YOU IN PEACE, TO OVERWHELM YOU WITH MY NEVER-ENDING, ALL-CONSUMING LOVE. I AM YOURS AND YOU ARE MINE.

LOVE ALWAYS,

YOUR DADDY GOD

SWEET, SWEET DAUGHTER,

LET GO OF IT ALL AND LET ME WORK. LET ME MOVE ON YOUR BEHALF TO SET YOU FREE. LET ME HEAL YOU, DELIVER YOU, RESTORE YOU TO WHAT I CREATED YOU TO BE. YOU ARE BEAUTIFUL TO ME, MY CHILD. I CREATED YOU WITH SUCH A PURPOSE. MY PLANS FOR YOU ARE SO GREAT! LET ME WALK YOU AWAY FROM ALL THE PAIN AND SORROW YOU ARE CARRYING. YOU ARE NOT MEANT TO CARRY ALL OF THAT. I CAN HANDLE IT, AND I CAN MAKE ALL THINGS NEW, MY BELOVED. WILL YOU TRUST ME WITH ALL OF YOU? I WILL NEVER LEAVE YOU OR HARM YOU. I PROMISE YOU THAT, MY DAUGHTER. I LOVE YOU MORE THAN YOU CAN EVEN IMAGINE. I LOVE YOU!

LOVE ALWAYS,

YOUR PAPA GOD
YOUR EVERYTHING

MY BELOVED,

YOU ARE SO PRECIOUS TO ME IN SO MANY WAYS. I DELIGHT IN YOU, MY CHILD. I AM VERY, VERY PLEASED WITH YOU. YOU SHINE MY LIGHT TO OTHERS, AND YOU SHOW THEM THE WAY TO ME. YOU ARE FILLED WITH MY PRESENCE, AND IT SPILLS OUT TO THOSE AROUND YOU. YOU HAVE A PASSION AND A HUNGER FOR ME AND FOR MY LOST AND HURTING CHILDREN. I AM NOT FINISHED WITH YOU, MY DELIGHTFUL GIRL. I HAVE SO MUCH TO SHOW YOU AND FOR US TO DO TOGETHER. FATHER AND DAUGHTER TOGETHER! CONTINUE TO SOAK IN ME, MY CHILD, AND LET ME FILL YOU TO OVERFLOWING. LET ME WASH AWAY THE WORLD AND ALL ITS TROUBLE.

LOVE ALWAYS,

YOUR DADDY
YOUR BEST FRIEND

BEAUTIFUL DAUGHTER,

YOU ARE MINE. YOU HAVE ALWAYS BEEN AND ALWAYS WILL BE MINE. I TREASURE YOU, CHERISH YOU, ADORE YOU! YOU ARE MY BEAUTIFUL INSIDE AND OUT GIRL, AND I JUST WANT TO SHOW YOU OFF. KEEP SMILING AND SHOWING MY LIGHT TO THOSE AROUND YOU. YOU ARE A WALKING TESTIMONY OF MY LOVE AND RESTORATION. I HAVE CREATED YOU WITH PURPOSE, MY PURPOSE. YOU HAVE BEEN IN A FIERCE BATTLE, BUT TOGETHER WE STAND STRONG, AND THE ENEMY CANNOT DEFEAT YOU! PUT ON YOUR ARMOR AND STAND STRONG, MY BELOVED. STAND STRONG IN ME. WE ARE A MIGHTY FORCE, YOU AND I.

I LOVE YOU, LOVE YOU, LOVE YOU.

YOUR PAPA GOD
YOUR DELIVERER

MY BELOVED,

OH, HOW I LOVE AND CHERISH YOU, MY DAUGHTER. YOU BLESS ME WITH YOUR PASSION AND LOVE FOR ME AND FOR THOSE AROUND YOU. KEEP GOING, MY SWEET DAUGHTER. KEEP GOING WITH ME BY YOUR SIDE. I WILL NEVER LEAVE YOU OR FORSAKE YOU. NEVER! YOU ARE TOO PRECIOUS AND VALUABLE TO ME. I AM WALKING BY YOUR SIDE AT ALL TIMES. I HAVE SO MUCH TO SHOW YOU, TO SHARE WITH YOU. TAKE MY HAND AND DO NOT LET GO. THIS IS A PATH AND A JOURNEY THAT WE ARE WALKING TOGETHER. HAND IN HAND WE GO, FATHER AND DAUGHTER TOGETHER. WHAT A BEAUTIFUL JOURNEY IT WILL BE!

LOVE ALWAYS,

YOUR PAPA GOD
YOUR REDEEMER

MY AMAZING SON,

I AM VERY PLEASED WITH YOU. YOU BRING A SMILE TO MY FACE WHEN I THINK OF YOU - YOUR SERVANT'S HEART, YOUR COMPASSION, YOUR WILLINGNESS TO HELP OTHERS AT A MOMENT'S NOTICE. YOU REFLECT ME IN ALL THAT YOU DO. I AM ONE PROUD PAPA! KEEP SUBMITTING TO ME EACH AND EVERY DAY. I AM ALWAYS LOOKING FOR THOSE WHO ARE AVAILABLE AND THOSE THAT ARE LISTENING FOR MY VOICE. YOU ARE MY CHOSEN ONE, MY FAVORITE, MY BELOVED CHILD. THANK YOU FOR LOVING ME THE WAY YOU DO AND TELLING OTHERS HOW MUCH I LOVE THEM. THERE ARE SO MANY LOST AND HURTING OUT THERE, AND I NEED YOU TO REACH OUT AND SHOW THEM THE WAY TO ME AND MY SALVATION. DO NOT WORRY AND DO NOT DOUBT THAT I AM PROVIDING FOR YOU AND YOUR FAMILY IN ALL WAYS. CAST YOUR CARES ON ME AND LET ME RESCUE

YOU AND FILL YOU WITH PEACE, MY PEACE THAT PASSES ALL UNDERSTANDING. I PROMISED THAT I WOULD ALWAYS BE RIGHT BY YOUR SIDE. I AM SO CLOSE TO YOU THAT YOU CAN REACH OUT AND TOUCH ME. KNOW THAT EVEN WHEN YOU DO NOT SENSE MY PRESENCE WITH YOU, I AM STILL ALWAYS RIGHT THERE GUIDING AND PROTECTING YOU AT EVERY TURN. YOU DO NOT HAVE TO FEAR. I LOVE YOU MORE THAN YOU CAN POSSIBLY IMAGINE. MY LOVE SURROUNDS YOU ON EVERY SIDE. I PROMISE!

LOVE NEVER-ENDING,

YOUR PROUD PAPA
YOUR SAVIOR
YOUR ALL IN ALL

MY BEAUTIFUL CHILD,

YOU ARE MINE AND I AM YOURS ALWAYS AND FOREVER. I WANT YOU TO BE FREE. I WANT YOU TO FLY, MY WARRIOR. THIS IS YOUR DAY OF FREEDOM, DAY ONE. I AM WORKING IN YOU AND THROUGH YOU TO BRING GLORY TO MY NAME. I DO NOT WANT YOU TO STRUGGLE AND BE WORN OUT, MY CHILD. I WANT YOU TO LET ME CARRY YOU THROUGH IT ALL. JUST LET ME CARRY YOU. YOU ARE SO PRECIOUS TO ME. I LOVE YOU MORE THAN WORDS COULD EVER SAY. YOU HAVE BEEN BOUGHT WITH A PRICE, AND YOU HAVE BEEN CHOSEN BY ME, AND I CHOOSE YOU OVER AND OVER AGAIN. THAT IS HOW IMPORTANT YOU ARE TO ME. PLEASE ALWAYS REMEMBER THAT. I AM ALWAYS ALWAYS HERE WITH YOU – GUARDING YOU, PROTECTING YOU, LOVING YOU.

LOVE ALWAYS,

YOUR DADDY GOD

SWEET CHILD OF MINE,

I AM YOURS AND YOU ARE MINE. THERE IS NO OTHER BEFORE ME, MY DAUGHTER. I AM ALL YOU NEED, SO SEEK AFTER ME WITH YOUR WHOLE UNDIVIDED HEART. LET ME GUIDE YOU EVERY SINGLE STEP THAT YOU TAKE. I AM THE VERY BREATH IN YOUR LUNGS. I AM EVERY BEAT OF YOUR HEART. I AM LIFE, FREEDOM, JOY, PEACE - EVERYTHING YOU ARE LONGING FOR AND SEEKING AFTER. I CREATED YOU TO LOVE - NOT ONLY ME, BUT THOSE AROUND YOU. LET ME PUT A SMILE ON YOUR FACE THAT DRAWS OTHERS TO ME. LET ME FILL YOU WITH SUCH COMPASSION. LET ME LIGHTEN EVERY STEP YOU TAKE SO YOU CAN WALK ABOVE THE CARES OF THE WORLD. LET ME FILL YOU WITH SUCH PASSION FOR ME THAT NOTHING ELSE MATTERS. I WANT ALL OF THIS FOR YOU, FOR US, MY BRIDE.

I LOVE YOU!

YOUR REDEEMER
YOUR SAFE PLACE

I AM HERE, MY DAUGHTER, I AM HERE. JUST MELT INTO MY ARMS AND LET ME TAKE EVERYTHING AWAY FROM YOU. ALL OF THE HEAVINESS, THE BURDEN, THE STRESS, THE TOO MUCH TO HANDLE. I DO NOT WANT YOU TO BE WALKING THROUGH ALL OF THIS. IT IS NOT MY PLAN FOR YOU. I CREATED YOU TO BE IN PEACE, TO FEEL THE JOY I HAVE FOR YOU. LET ME CARRY YOU, MY BELOVED. YOU ARE PRECIOUS TO ME, AND AS YOUR DADDY, I AM HERE TO PROTECT YOU ON ALL SIDES. I AM COVERING YOU WITH MY PRESENCE. I AM YOUR SAFE PLACE. JUST STAY WITH ME, REST IN ME, AND CONTINUALLY BE WITH ME. THE WORLD CAN BE HARSH, BUT YOU ARE NOT OF THIS WORLD. YOU ARE SET APART FOR ME.

I LOVE YOU ALWAYS,

YOUR PROUD PAPA
YOUR COMFORTER

MY INCREDIBLE CHILD,

YOU ARE BEAUTIFUL TO ME IN EVERY WAY. I CREATED YOU TO LOVE, DANCE, SING, HEAL OTHERS, BUT FIRST LET ME HEAL YOUR HEART. YOU HAVE WALKED THROUGH A LOT OF PAIN. I HAVE SEEN YOUR TEARS, YOUR CRIES. LET ME JUST HOLD YOU IN MY ARMS AND LOVE THE HURT AWAY. YOU ARE SO VERY PRECIOUS TO ME, MY BELOVED. YOU ARE MINE AND I AM YOURS. YOU ARE A LIGHT IN THE DARKNESS THAT LEADS THE LOST AND HURTING TO ME. LET ME REIGNITE YOU, LET ME USE YOU LIKE NEVER BEFORE. LET MY PASSION BURN IN YOU AT A LEVEL YOU HAVE NEVER EXPERIENCED BEFORE.

LOVE ALWAYS,

YOUR PAPA GOD
YOUR FLAME

MY PRECIOUS DAUGHTER,

I DELIGHT IN YOU, MY BELOVED. OH, HOW I DELIGHT IN EVERYTHING ABOUT YOU. YOUR SMILE, YOUR PASSION AND COMPASSION, YOUR GENEROSITY AND CARING. YOU REFLECT ME TO OTHERS, AND I AM SO VERY VERY PLEASED WITH YOU. KEEP WALKING ONE STEP AT A TIME WITH ME, MY FAITHFUL ONE. DO NOT LOOK BEHIND YOU, BESIDE YOU, OR IN FRONT OF YOU. KEEP YOUR EYES FULLY FOCUSED ON ME AT ALL TIMES AND LET ME TAKE YOU WHERE I HAVE CALLED YOU TO GO. THERE CAN BE MANY DISTRACTIONS IN THIS WORLD, SO THAT IS WHY YOU NEED TO KEEP YOUR FOCUS ON ME, ON US. I HAVE MORE AND MORE FOR YOU, MY DAUGHTER, BUT ALWAYS REMEMBER - ONE STEP AT A TIME. MY PLANS AND MY TIMING ARE PERFECT.

I LOVE YOU!

YOUR FAITHFUL FATHER
YOUR DELIVERER

MY PRECIOUS DAUGHTER,

OH, HOW I DELIGHT IN YOU. I LOVE YOUR SMILE, I LOVE YOUR HEART, AND YOUR LOVE FOR OTHERS. I LOVE HOW YOU TAKE CARE OF MY CREATION. YOU ARE A FAITHFUL SHEPHERD AND GUARDIAN TO MANY. I CREATED YOU TO POUR INTO OTHERS AND TO POINT THEM TO ME. I AM WELL PLEASED WITH YOU, MY BELOVED DAUGHTER OF MINE. I HAVE SO MUCH FOR YOU TO DO, FOR US TO DO TOGETHER. LET ME CONTINUE TO MOLD YOU AND MAKE YOU EXACTLY WHO I HAVE CREATED YOU TO BE. THERE HAVE BEEN ROCKS ON YOUR PATH THAT HAVE CAUSED YOU TO STUMBLE AND LOSE YOUR WAY, BUT I AM ALWAYS HERE RIGHT BESIDE YOU TO MAKE YOUR PATH STRAIGHT AND SMOOTH AGAIN. JUST LEAN ON ME AND LET ME GUIDE YOU AND DIRECT YOU. WE ARE WALKING THIS PATH TOGETHER. YOU ARE NEVER EVER ALONE. I PROMISE YOU THAT. I PROMISED TO NEVER LEAVE YOU OR FORSAKE YOU, AND I NEVER WILL. YOU CAN TRUST ME TO ALWAYS BE THERE FIGHTING FOR YOU.
I LOVE YOU MORE THAN YOU HAVE EVEN IMAGINE.

LOVE NEVER-ENDING,

YOUR FAITHFUL PAPA
YOUR EVERYTHING

MY PRECIOUS SON,

I LOVE YOU SO MUCH! I ALWAYS HAVE AND I ALWAYS WILL. I AM RIGHT HERE BY YOUR SIDE, MY BELOVED CHILD. YOU CAN TRUST ME TO NEVER WALK AWAY FROM YOU. YOU ARE MUCH TOO IMPORTANT TO ME. I MADE A PROMISE TO YOU IN MY WORD TO NEVER LEAVE YOU. I HAVE SEEN YOUR SORROW AND YOUR PAIN. I HAVE SHED TEARS RIGHT ALONGSIDE YOU. I AM HERE TO BRING YOU PEACE, FREEDOM, A LOVE THAT YOU HAVE NEVER FELT BEFORE. LET ME WORK, MY SON. HOLD NOTHING BACK AND LET ME DO A MIGHTY WORK IN YOU. I AM THE POTTER AND YOU ARE THE CLAY, SO PLEASE LET ME MOLD YOU AND SHAPE YOU INTO WHO I CREATED YOU TO BE! WE HAVE SO MUCH TO DO TOGETHER, MANY PEOPLE TO REACH AND HELP. I HAVE CREATED YOU WITH A COMPASSION AND A LOVE FOR OTHERS THAT REFLECTS ME TO THEM. SOME OF THE ONES I WANT YOU TO SPEAK TO WILL SEE ME FOR THE FIRST TIME THROUGH YOU. YOU ARE MY CHOSEN VESSEL. TODAY IS THE FIRST DAY OF A NEW JOURNEY FOR US. SURRENDER ALL AND LET ME HEAL YOU AND RESTORE YOU.

LOVE ALWAYS,

YOUR REDEEMER
YOUR HEALER

MY SWEET GIRL,

LET ME HOLD YOU, LET ME LOVE ON YOU. LET ME ROCK AWAY THE CARES OF THIS WORLD AND THE HEAVINESS THAT HAS SURROUNDED YOU, MY BELOVED. LET ME HEAL YOUR HURTS AND YOUR WOUNDS. LET ME SURROUND YOU WITH MY PERFECT PEACE. YOU ARE MY DELIGHT AND MY JOY. YOU ARE MINE AND I AM YOURS. I AM ALWAYS HERE. I PROMISE YOU THAT. YOU ARE NEVER EVER ALONE. I AM HERE TO PROTECT YOU ON ALL SIDES WHEN THE ENEMY OR THE WORLD TRIES TO COME AT YOU. MY ANGELS SURROUND YOU AND BATTLE FOR YOU. YOU ARE MINE, I SAY AGAIN. THE ENEMY CANNOT AND WILL NOT CONTINUE TO TORMENT YOU. THAT IS NOT MY PLAN AND THIS IS NOT MY WAY. YES, WE HAVE TROUBLES IN THIS WORLD, BUT I AM CALLING YOU AND POSITIONING YOU ABOVE IT ALL AS MY LIGHT, MY REPRESENTATIVE AND WITNESS IN THIS WORLD. SO, SHINE, MY DAUGHTER, SHINE! YOU ARE A DIAMOND IN THE ROUGH, A LIGHT IN THE DARKNESS. YOU ARE FREE!

LOVE NEVER-ENDING,

YOUR PAPA GOD
YOUR REDEEMER
YOUR HOPE

MY SWEET DAUGHTER,

I LOVE YOU, I LOVE YOU, I LOVE YOU! YOU ARE MY TREASURE - SO VERY VERY PRECIOUS TO ME, MY BELOVED. I JUST WANT TO HOLD YOU, COMFORT YOU, LOVE ON YOU. CRAWL INTO MY LAP AND JUST STAY. CLOSE YOUR EYES AND REST. YOU ARE SAFE WITH ME. NOTHING WILL HARM YOU BECAUSE YOUR DADDY IS WATCHING OVER YOU. I AM GIVING YOU PEACE AND CALM. I AM PLACING IT ON YOU LIKE A BLANKET, MY SECURITY BLANKET. REST, MY DAUGHTER, REST. YOU HAVE BEEN THROUGH A BATTLE, AND IT IS TIME TO RECOVER. LET ME HEAL AND RESTORE YOU. LET ME DO A MIGHTY WORK IN YOU TO PREPARE YOU FOR THE NEXT STEP IN OUR JOURNEY. I AM RESTORING YOUR STRENGTH; I AM RESTORING YOUR ARMOR. I AM FILLING YOU WITH ME SO NOTHING OF THE WORLD CAN REMAIN. OH, MY PRECIOUS BEAUTIFUL CHOSEN ONE, YOU ARE MINE AND I AM YOURS. ALWAYS!

LOVE FOREVER,
YOUR REDEEMER
YOUR COMFORTER
YOUR ALL IN ALL

MY LOVE FOR YOU IS NEVER-ENDING. IT SURROUNDS AND PROTECTS YOU FROM ALL THE ARROWS SLUNG IN YOUR DIRECTION. YOU DO NOT EVEN KNOW OF MOST OF THE ATTACKS THAT ARE DIRECTED TOWARDS YOU BECAUSE I STOP THEM. I WANT PEACE FOR YOU - ALL-CONSUMING, NEVER-ENDING PEACE AT ALL TIMES. LET ME CALM YOUR MIND AND BODY. REST IN ME, CLING TO ME, LET ME HOLD YOU AND ROCK YOU INTO A SWEET PLACE WHERE IT IS JUST THE TWO OF US TOGETHER. NO INTERRUPTIONS, NO DISTRACTIONS. NOTHING BUT US. I AM ALL YOU NEED. WHEN YOU REST COMPLETELY IN ME, THEN THE STUFF OF LIFE DOES NOT OVERWHELM OR BOTHER YOU. THE JOYS OF LIFE ARE ALWAYS PRESENT. THIS IS MY PERFECT PLACE FOR YOU - JOY AND PEACE. HOW I LOVE TO GIVE MY CHILDREN GOOD THINGS. I AM A GENEROUS DADDY. I DO NOT WITHHOLD GOOD FROM MY CHILDREN. JUST ASK FOR WHAT YOU NEED. IT IS ALREADY YOURS. I AM JUST WAITING FOR YOU TO ASK. CALL ON ME AND I WILL ANSWER ALWAYS.

LOVE,

YOUR PROVIDER
YOUR PERFECT PEACE

MY BEAUTIFUL DAUGHTER,

I SEE YOU, I KNOW YOU, I LOVE YOU MORE THAN YOU CAN IMAGINE. I SEE YOUR HEART, YOUR PASSION, YOUR COMPASSION, YOUR GENTLENESS. I SEE SUCH BEAUTY, INSIDE AND OUT, MY BELOVED. I FEEL YOUR DOUBT AND YOUR STRUGGLES, BUT YOU DO NOT NEED TO STRUGGLE WITH ME. YOU ALREADY HAVE MY LOVE. THERE ISN'T ANYTHING YOU NEED TO DO TO EARN MORE. MY LOVE FOR YOU IS NEVER-ENDING. IT SURROUNDS YOU EVERY SECOND OF EVERY MINUTE OF EVERY DAY. I PROMISED IN MY WORD THAT I WOULD NEVER LEAVE YOU OR FORSAKE YOU. I NEVER WILL. I AM YOUR EVER-PRESENT HELP IN TIME OF NEED. I AM YOUR COMFORTER AND YOUR HEALER. I AM ALL THAT YOU NEED, MY CHILD. SEEK ME ALWAYS. RUN INTO MY ARMS AND JUST SIT. I GIVE YOU MY PEACE THAT PASSES ALL UNDERSTANDING. A PEACE THAT IS LIKE NO OTHER. A PEACE THAT YOU CARRY WITH YOU WHEREVER YOU GO. TRUST ME, MY PRECIOUS, PRECIOUS DAUGHTER. I WILL NEVER HURT YOU OR ABANDON YOU. I AM NEVER TOO BUSY TO BE WITH YOU. I AM ALWAYS RIGHT HERE WITH YOU. ALWAYS.

LOVE NEVER-ENDING,

YOUR PAPA GOD
YOUR EVERYTHING
YOUR DELIVERER
YOUR REDEEMER

I AM SO PLEASED WITH YOU. I DELIGHT IN
YOU, BEAUTIFUL ONE. THANK YOU FOR GIVING
ME YOUR HEART AND YOUR LIFE. I HAVE BEEN
WITH YOU FROM THE VERY BEGINNING. NOW,
WE CAN SPEND TIME TOGETHER AS ONE. I
HAVE BEEN LONGING FOR YOU, FOR US TO BE
TOGETHER, AND NOW WE CAN. I LOVE YOU
BEYOND WORDS. YOU ARE SO PRECIOUS TO
ME. OUR JOURNEY IS JUST BEGINNING. YOU
AND ME WALKING HAND IN HAND ALONG THE
PATH I AM LAYING OUT BEFORE YOU. A PATH
OF PEACE FOR YOU AND YOUR CHILDREN. KEEP
YOUR EYES ON ME AT ALL TIMES. I WILL
NEVER LEAD YOU ASTRAY. MY PLANS FOR YOU
ARE TO PROSPER YOU AND NOT TO HARM YOU.
I BRING YOU A HOPE AND A FUTURE. WE HAVE
MANY THINGS TO DO TOGETHER, MY BELOVED.
LIVE A LIFE OF CONTINUAL SURRENDER. IF
SOMEONE OFFENDS YOU - FORGIVE THEM.
LOVE ALWAYS. I AM LOVE AND I WANT THEM
TO SEE LOVE IN YOU AND THROUGH YOU.

LOVE ALWAYS,

YOUR PAPA GOD
YOUR DELIGHT
YOUR FOREVER LOVE

PRECIOUS GIRL OF MINE,

I LOVE YOU! I LOVE YOUR SMILE, YOUR JOY. YOU HAVE EMBRACED ME IN SUCH A BEAUTIFUL WAY, AND YOU ARE CHANGING YOUR WORLD. NOW LET US WORK TOGETHER TO CHANGE OTHER'S WORLDS. LET ME FILL YOU WITH SO MUCH PEACE THAT IT JUST FLOWS OUT OF YOU TO THOSE AROUND YOU. LET ME FILL YOU WITH SUCH LIGHT, MY LIGHT, THAT YOU GLOW FOR ME AND DRAW OTHERS TO ME. SURRENDER ALL AND WATCH ME MOVE. YOU HAVE COME SO FAR ALREADY. I HAVE MANY, MANY PLANS FOR THE TWO OF US, MY BELOVED. I AM PLEASED WITH YOU, MY SWEET GIRL. I AM ONE PROUD PAPA WANTING TO SHOW OFF HIS BEAUTIFUL GIRL. WHEREVER YOU GO YOU ARE REFLECTING ME. PEOPLE ARE HUNGRY FOR WHAT YOU HAVE. SHARE FULLY ALL I HAVE DONE FOR YOU SO THAT OTHERS FIND ME. THANK YOU FOR YOUR WILLINGNESS TO LET ME WORK IN YOU AND THROUGH YOU. THANK YOU.

LOVE ALWAYS,

YOUR PAPA GOD
YOUR BELOVED
YOUR EVERYTHING

I pray that these letters speak to you. God's living Word is eternal, and I believe that these letters are eternal as well. They have no expiration date. You can read them over and over again, and the message, God's love for you, never changes.

Ephesians 3:16-18: I pray that out of His glorious riches He may strengthen you with power through His Spirit in your inner being, so that Christ may dwell in your hearts through faith. And I pray that you, being rooted and established in love, may have power, together with all the Lord's holy people, to grasp how wide and long and high and deep is the love of Christ, and to know this love that surpasses knowledge - that you may be filled to the measure of all the fullness of God.

I love how the Lord even quotes His own written Word in these letters. His Word is love, and these letters are so full of love as well.

There are different types of prophetic words that are given. Some are a call to action or repentance. Some talk of judgment. Some, like these letters, are full of encouragement, mercy, love, and a hopeful future. These are sometimes called words of edification. Prophesy should always line up with scripture. If a prophesy contradicts who God is or what His Word says then I would say it is not true prophesy.

I talked a little about the way God created me to be a scribe, transcriptionist, or a recorder of words. The words in these letters are not mine. If you asked me something about these letters later, I could not tell you what was in them. They are "downloaded" from Holy Spirit, and they are His words, not mine. I do not claim them as my own, and I am truly humbled to be used by God in such a beautiful way. I thank Him every day for the privilege of being His scribe.

Here are some of the scripture references of verses from the Bible that the Lord uses in these letters:

Song of Solomon 6:3 - I am fully devoted to my beloved, and my beloved is fully devoted to me.

Hebrews 13:5 - ….for hasn;t He promised you "I will never leave you, never! And I will not loosen my grip on your life!"

I am including some of the prophetic words Papa God has given to the church or on social media. Some are a call to repentance, some are words to stir His people to action, some are also love letters of sorts for a bigger audience. This is an area that the Lord placed me in a few years ago to grow and stretch me. Again, I am a fully surrendered vessel, and He speaks to His children through the words He gives me. I am in awe of the different ways that He speaks. Very often, I am in worship or prayer and the words just start flowing! I have to grab a notepad or my phone to start recording what Papa God wants to say to His people. I have learned to keep a pen and paper in several rooms of the house so I am ready to receive what He is saying. I am humbled that He chooses to speak through Me. These are the same as the love letters in that you choose to receive the words and take them as your own. The word that is given may be for one specific person or an entire group of people. I have had people come up to me after church and thank me for the word I shared. I used to be uncomfortable receiving thanks, but I thank Papa God for using me to deliver his love and direction. It is truly a blessing in so many ways.

Prophetic Words

LISTEN MY CHILDREN, PLEASE LISTEN. I HAVE TOLD YOU TIME AND TIME AGAIN TO TAKE YOUR EYES OFF THE WORLD AND LOOK ONLY TO ME. THIS IS EVEN MORE IMPORTANT NOW THAN IT HAS EVER BEEN BEFORE. THE WORLD IS IN CHAOS, BUT I AM NOT CHAOS. THE WORLD IS IN FEAR, BUT I AM NOT FEAR. I AM PEACE. I AM THE CALM, YOUR CALM, IN THE STORM. I AM THE ONE THAT BRINGS ORDER. I AM THE ONE WHO DELIVERS YOU AND SETS YOUR FEET ON SOLID GROUND. I AM THE ONE WHO FILLS YOU WITH MY PRESENCE SO YOU CAN DO EVEN GREATER WORKS. EVEN NOW, I AM MOLDING YOU AND SHAPING YOU INTO WHAT I CREATED YOU TO BE FOR THIS TIME. I AM THE POTTER, AND YOU ARE THE CLAY. ALL OF THIS MOLDING AND SHAPING CAN BE UNCOMFORTABLE AT TIMES, BUT IT IS OH SO NECESSARY, MY CHILDREN. I AM ASKING YOU TO TRUST ME AND LET ME WORK. I AM A GREAT AND MIGHTY GOD, BUT I AM ALSO A PATIENT AND GENTLE GOD. LET ME DO MY WORK IN YOU, MY CHILDREN. OH, PLEASE LET ME DO MY WORK IN YOU. LET GO OF CONTROL AND LET ME WORK. I WON'T FORCE YOU TO BE MOLDED, SO IF YOU SAY NO THEN IT IS NO. BUT OH, WHAT YOU WILL MISS IF YOU DON'T LET ME DO MY WORK IN YOU. I HAVE SO MUCH FOR YOU TO DO. SO MUCH FOR YOU TO BE IN ME. SO, AGAIN, I AM SAYING TAKE YOUR EYES OFF THE WORLD AROUND YOU AND JUST COME AWAY WITH ME. WON'T YOU COME AWAY WITH ME?

CAN YOU HEAR IT? ARE YOU LISTENING? CAN YOU HEAR ME ROAR? CAN YOU HEAR ME CRY OUT FOR MY PEOPLE TO UNITE? STAND FIRM AND STAND STRONG TOGETHER IN MY NAME AND IN MY STRENGTH! I AM CALLING YOU UP AND I AM CALLING YOU OUT! MY PEOPLE HAVE BEEN TREATED SO POORLY BUT NO MORE! I AM SAYING TO THE ENEMY GET YOUR HANDS OFF MY PEOPLE AND LET THEM GO! I AM HERE TO RESTORE ALL THAT THE ENEMY HAS STOLEN FROM YOU. I AM HERE TO BRING YOU JUSTICE AND TO REVIVE YOU, MY CHILDREN. THIS HAS BEEN A DIFFICULT SEASON TO WALK THROUGH, BUT I HAVE NEVER LEFT YOUR SIDE AND I NEVER WILL. I HAVE HEARD YOUR CRIES AND I HAVE FELT YOUR FEAR AND PAIN. I HAVE WALKED EVERY STEP RIGHT BESIDE YOU, EVEN WHEN YOU COULD NOT FEEL ME AND EVEN QUESTIONED IF I WAS THERE. I WAS THERE, MY SON. I WAS THERE, MY DAUGHTER. I NEVER LEFT YOUR SIDE AND I STAYED RIGHT BESIDE YOU ALL THE TIME. I AM STILL HERE. I AM HERE TO GIVE YOU A HOPE AND A FUTURE IN ME. SO, STEP OUT OF THE MESS, LET GO OF THE ANGER AND BITTERNESS OVER ALL OF THE INJUSTICE THAT HAS BEEN DONE. CHOOSE FAITH, CHOOSE JOY, CHOOSE LOVE AND PEACE. MY WAYS ARE HIGHER, SO WALK THE PATH THAT I AM LAYING BEFORE YOU. COME UP HIGHER WITH ME. TAKE YOUR FOCUS OFF THE WORLD AND LOOK ONLY TO ME. I AM YOUR REDEEMER. I AM YOUR DELIVERER. I AM YOUR EVERYTHING. I AM.

THE LORD SAYS YOU ARE MY CHOSEN PEOPLE, MY REMNANT. I HAVE SET YOU APART FOR SUCH A TIME AS THIS TO STAND STRONG, BE BOLD, TO SWING YOUR MIGHTY SWORD IN MY NAME, AND TO SEND THE ENEMY RUNNING. STAND UNWAVERING IN MY STRENGTH, IN MY POWER, IN MY MIGHT! STAND STRONG AGAINST THE EVIL IN THIS WORLD AND THE SCHEMES OF THE ENEMY. YOU ARE VICTORIOUS THROUGH ME. I AM LOOKING FOR PEOPLE WHO WILL BE MY WARRIORS AND MY CONQUERORS. I AM LOOKING FOR THOSE WHO WILL BE MY LIGHT AND WILL NOT BACK DOWN BECAUSE I AM IN YOU. I AM WITH YOU, I AM FOR YOU! SO, STAND UP, MY CHILDREN, AND BE COUNTED IN MY ARMY. STAND UP AND DO NOT BE AFRAID - FOR I AM YOUR SOURCE AND YOUR STRENGTH. I SEND MY ANGELS WITH YOU TO WIN THE BATTLE. CALL ON THEM BECAUSE THEY PROTECT YOU ON ALL SIDES. YES, THE BATTLE IS RAGING ALL AROUND YOU, BUT YOU ARE VICTORIOUS IN MY NAME! YOU ARE!! THE ENEMY WILL TRY TO THROW ALL SORTS OF THINGS YOUR WAY BUT STAND STRONG. HE HAS ALREADY LOST, AND HE KNOWS HIS FATE. COVER YOURSELF WITH THE ARMOR AND PLEAD THE BLOOD, MY SON'S POWERFUL BLOOD, ALL OVER YOU AND YOUR FAMILY. DO NOT FEAR. FEAR IS NOT OF ME. STAND FIRM IN YOUR FAITH WITH YOUR FEET PLANTED. THE BATTLE HAS BEEN WON. THE BATTLE HAS BEEN WON!

INCREASE INCREASE INCREASE! CALL OUT FOR THE INCREASE, MY INCREASE! INCREASED FIRE, INCREASED ANOINTING, INCREASED POWER! I AM POURING IT DOWN ON YOU, MY CHILDREN. OPEN YOUR HANDS AND RECEIVE IT. MORE OF ME IN EVERY AREA. THIS IS THE TIME TO RECEIVE IT AND RELEASE IT TO THOSE AROUND YOU. MY DESIRE FOR YOU IS MORE. MORE OF EVERYTHING I HAVE FOR YOU. IF YOU ARE HUNGRY FOR MORE THAN ALL YOU HAVE TO DO IS RECEIVE IT. BUT DON'T JUST KEEP IT FOR YOURSELF. LET ME USE YOUR HANDS, YOUR FEET, YOUR MOUTH, YOUR HEART. BE MY YIELDED VESSELS AND LET THEM SEE ME IN YOU! THIS WORLD IS SEARCHING FOR ANSWERS, AND I AM THE ANSWER. THIS WORLD IS LONGING FOR COMFORT, AND I AM THAT COMFORT. THIS WORLD IS LOOKING FOR PURPOSE, AND I AM THAT PURPOSE! I HAVE COME THAT THEY MAY HAVE LIFE AND HAVE IT IN ABUNDANCE, SO BE ME IN THIS WORLD. SHOW ME TO THIS WORLD. I AM ALL THAT THEY NEED AND ALL THAT THEY WILL EVER NEED. I AM!

STEP INTO THE FLOW, MY CHILDREN. MY FLOW OF LIVING HEALING WATER. STEP INTO THE WATER AND GO DEEPER AND DEEPER. DO NOT BE AFRAID OF MY POWER. OPEN UP TO IT AND JUST KEEP WALKING. DO NOT STOP AT YOUR KNEES, OR YOUR HIPS, OR EVEN YOUR SHOULDERS. SURRENDER ALL AND JUST GO UNDER. GIVE IT ALL TO ME AND BE RESTORED, REFRESHED, AND RENEWED, MY BELOVED. GO ALL THE WAY UNDER AND LET ME FILL YOU TO OVERFLOWING! NEW BAPTISM, NEW FIRE, NEW PASSION. NEW PURPOSE, AND NEW DIRECTION. OH, GIVE IT ALL TO ME. HOLD NOTHING BACK. YOU CAN TRUST ME TO MAKE ALL THINGS NEW! YES, MY CHILDREN, I MAKE ALL THINGS NEW!

THE DAYS OF LUKEWARM ARE OVER. THE DAYS OF WALKING THE LINE ARE THROUGH. THE DAYS OF ONE FOOT IN THE WORLD AND ONE FOOT AT THE CROSS CANNOT CONTINUE. CHOOSE THIS DAY WHOM YOU WILL SERVE. I AM LOOKING FOR A BRIDE WHO IS ON FIRE FOR ME! I AM LOOKING FOR A CHURCH WHO WILL GIVE IT ALL TO ME! I AM LOOKING FOR A PEOPLE WHO WILL GO TO THE FRONT LINES AND FIGHT IN MY NAME. THE DAYS OF PLAYING CHURCH ARE DONE. PUT ON YOUR WHOLE ARMOR AND LET'S GO INTO BATTLE! WHERE ARE THE ONES WHO WILL STAND AND BE COUNTED AMONGST THE FAITHFUL? WHO ARE THE ONES THAT WILL FIGHT FOR MY PEOPLE? MANY ARE CALLED BUT FEW WILL ANSWER. MANY WILL START THE JOURNEY, BUT FEW WILL FINISH. BE THE ONE THAT GOES THE DISTANCE WITH ME. THE ONE WHO DOESN'T GROW WEARY IN THE BATTLE. THE ONE WHO CALLS ON MY STRENGTH. BE WHO I CALLED YOU TO BE.

MY CHILDREN, I HAVE HEARD YOUR CRIES, YOUR PLEAS, YOUR DESPERATION THROUGH THIS DIFFICULT SEASON. I HAVE NOT IGNORED YOU OR TURNED AWAY. I HAVE ALWAYS BEEN HERE. I AM ALWAYS, ALWAYS HERE. I DO NOT SLUMBER; I DO NOT REST. I HAVE NOT FORSAKEN YOU. I HAVE BEEN WORKING THINGS OUT FOR YOUR GOOD, MY BELOVED. I HAVE SENT MY ANGELS TO GUARD YOU AND TO FIGHT FOR YOU. I HAVE PUT PEOPLE IN YOUR PATH TO PRAY WITH YOU AND TO SPEAK LIFE INTO YOU. I HAVE SENT PROVISION, EVEN WHEN IT DIDN'T LOOK LIKE IT. I HAVE BROUGHT YOU HOPE WHEN THINGS HAVE LOOKED HOPELESS. I KNOW IT STILL LOOKS DARK, BUT LIGHT IS BREAKING ALL AROUND YOU! THIS IS A SEASON OF SIGNS, MIRACLES, AND WONDERS! THIS IS A TIME OF BREAKTHROUGH! THIS IS WHAT YOU HAVE BEEN LONGING FOR, MY SAINTS. LOOK ALL AROUND YOU AND SEE ME AT WORK! TAKE YOUR EYES OFF THE WORLD AND FOCUS ON ME, ON WHAT I AM DOING. HOW I AM MOVING ON YOUR BEHALF. THE SEASON OF SORROW IS OVER, AND THE SEASON OF REJOICING IS HERE!

I AM HERE, MY CHILDREN, STIRRING UP THE ATMOSPHERE. EVERYTHING IS SHIFTING, EVERYTHING IS CHANGING. CAN YOU FEEL IT? CAN YOU FEEL MY HOLY SPIRIT ALL AROUND YOU? INVITE ME IN, OPEN THE DOOR OF YOUR HEART, AND WELCOME ME IN, THE KING OF KINGS AND THE LORD OF LORDS. YOU ARE THE ONE I LOVE. YOU ARE THE ONE I ADORE. YOU ARE THE ONE I LONG FOR, MY BELOVED. DO YOU LONG FOR ME? DO YOU HUNGER FOR ME? LET GO AND LET ME DO A MIGHTY WORK IN YOU. LET ME IGNITE A CLEANSING FIRE IN YOU. LET ME RESTORE YOU. REVIVAL STARTS IN YOU. RESTORATION STARTS IN YOU. REDEMPTION STARTS IN YOU. COME TO THE ALTAR AND SURRENDER ALL. FALL TO YOUR KNEES AND CRY OUT TO ME. LET IT START WITH YOU, THE ONE I LOVE AND HAVE BEEN LONGING FOR. LET IT START WITH YOU!

I AM THE GOD WHO HEALS. I AM THE GOD WHO RESTORES. I AM THE GOD WHO RESCUES. I AM THE GOD WHO LIFTS YOU UP. I AM THE GOD WHO FIGHTS FOR YOU. I AM THE GOD WHO IS WITH YOU ALWAYS. I AM THE GOD WHO WILL NEVER LEAVE YOU OR FORSAKE YOU. SO, LOOK TO ME, RUN TO ME, CLING TO ME, BE WITH ME. I LONG FOR YOU, I HUNGER FOR YOU, I LOVE YOU! DO YOU HUNGER FOR ME? DO YOU LONG FOR ME? COME AWAY WITH ME, MY BELOVED, AND LET US BE TOGETHER. LET ME POUR INTO YOU LIKE YOU HAVE NEVER EXPERIENCED BEFORE. LET ME OVERFLOW YOU WITH MY PEACE AND MY LOVE. LET ME WASH AWAY ALL FEAR, DOUBT, AND SADNESS. LET ME MAKE YOU NEW. OH, HOW I LONG TO MAKE YOU NEW. LET ME MOLD YOU AND MAKE YOU INTO WHO I HAVE ALWAYS WANTED YOU TO BE. WILL YOU LET ME?

THE TIME IS NOW! FREEDOM IS NOW! HEALING IS NOW! DELIVERANCE IS NOW! DO NOT HESITATE AND DO NOT WAIT FOR WHAT YOU FEEL IS THE PERFECT TIME, BECAUSE NOW IS THE TIME AND THIS IS THE PLACE! I AM RELEASING AN ANOINTING IN THE EARTH THAT IS MORE POWERFUL THAN HAS EVER BEEN FELT BEFORE! REACH OUT AND GRAB IT BECAUSE IT IS FOR ALL OF YOU AND NOT JUST A SELECT FEW. YOU ARE ALL MY CHOSEN, AND I LOVE YOU ALL AND WANT THIS ANOINTING TO FALL ON EVERY ONE OF YOU. SO, LIFT YOUR HANDS AND CALL DOWN MY RAIN TO FALL ON YOU AND TO CLEANSE YOU AND HEAL YOU AND GIVE YOU A CONNECTION AND CLOSENESS TO ME THAT YOU HAVE NEVER FELT BEFORE. IT IS HERE, IT IS HERE, IT IS HERE! MY ANOINTING IS HERE, AND IT IS FOR YOU! OPEN YOUR MOUTH AND RECEIVE IT AND LET ME DO A MIGHTY WORK IN YOU! LET ME FILL YOU TO OVERFLOWING! GIVE ME YOUR HANDS, YOUR FEET, YOUR MOUTH, YOUR SURRENDER. GIVE IT ALL TO ME AND WATCH ME WORK! I NEED YOU, I CHERISH YOU, I LOVE YOU! OH, HOW I LOVE YOU! IT BEGINS NOW!

AWAKEN FROM YOUR SLUMBER, MY CHILDREN, IT IS TIME TO WAKE UP. NO MORE STUMBLING IN THE DARK AND NO MORE WANDERING . I AM PUTTING EVERYTHING RIGHT! I AM CALLING MY LOST CHILDREN BACK TO ME. THOSE OF YOU WHO HAVE BEEN WALKING IN FEAR AND CONFUSION. THOSE OF YOU WHO HAVE BEEN LOOKING FOR DIRECTION IN YOUR LIFE. THOSE OF YOU WHO HAVE WALKED AWAY FROM THE PERFECT PLAN I HAVE FOR YOUR LIFE. THE TIME IS NOW TO RETURN HOME TO ME! STOP YOUR WANDERING AND RETURN HOME TO YOUR FATHER. YOUR FATHER, WHO LOVES, YOUR FATHER WHO PROMISES NEVER TO LEAVE YOU OR FORSAKE YOU. I AM THE WAY, THE TRUTH, AND THE LIGHT. OPEN YOUR EYES AND SEE THE TRUTH THAT I AM LAYING OUT BEFORE YOU. OPEN YOUR EARS AND LISTEN TO MY DIRECTIONS FOR YOU. OPEN YOUR MOUTH AND CRY OUT TO ME TO RESCUE YOU. NO MORE WANDERING, NO MORE DELAY, NO MORE CHAOS OR CONFUSION. I AM THE GOD OF PEACE, AND I AM THE GOD OF RESTORATION. I AM ALL THAT YOU WILL EVER NEED. I AM THE ONE WHO IS CALLING YOU HOME. I AM THE ONE WHO IS PULLING YOU OUT OF THE DARKNESS AND PLACING YOU IN THE LIGHT,

MY LIGHT. DO NOT BE AFRAID BECAUSE NOW IS THE TIME FOR THE RESTORATION OF MY PEOPLE. TURN AWAY FROM YOUR WICKED WAYS AND LET ME HEAL. YOU, RESTORE YOU, SET YOUR FEET ON SOLID GROUND. TRUST ME WITH ALL THAT YOU HAVE AND ALL THAT YOU ARE. TRUST ME WITH YOUR CHILDREN. I WILL NEVER HARM THEM. I LOVE THEM MORE THAN YOU CAN EVEN IMAGINE. SO DO NOT HESITATE, MY LOVE. RUN TO ME, RUN TO ME, RUN TO ME. FALL ON YOUR KNEES AND REPENT BEFORE ME, AND LET ME DO A MIGHTY WORK IN YOU. RESTORATION IS YOURS! RESTORATION IS YOURS!

MY CHILDREN, DO NOT BE AFRAID OF THE SHAKING. DO NOT BE AFRAID OF THE TURBULENCE IN THE ATMOSPHERE. IT IS NOT FOR THOSE WHO ARE WALKING WITH ME AND SERVING ME. THE TIME OF LUKEWARM IS OVER. THE TIME OF LIVING ONE WAY ON SUNDAY AND ANOTHER WAY THE REST OF THE WEEK IS DONE. I AM POURING OUT MY HOLY FIRE ON YOU, MY ANOINTING WILL KNOCK YOU OFF YOUR FEET. ELEVATION IS HERE! GRAB A HOLD OF IT, AND DON'T LET GO! THERE IS A BATTLE IN THE HEAVENLIES, BUT THERE IS ALSO A BATTLE ON THIS EARTH. EVIL HAS TRIED TO OVERTAKE MY PEOPLE, BUT I AM YOUR GOD, I AM HERE TO RESCUE AND DELIVER YOU. I AM HERE TO HEAL YOU AND SET YOU FREE. I AM HERE TO RESTORE YOU AND REPOSITION YOU. I AM HERE TO SET YOU ON FIRE FOR ME! I AM HERE TO CALL YOU HIGHER! I AM HERE TO CALL YOU OUT AS MY CHOSEN PEOPLE.

I AM STANDING OVER YOU, MY BELOVED. I AM LETTING OUT A ROAR THAT MAKES THE ENEMY SCATTER! I AM PIERCING THE DARKNESS WITH MY LIGHT. I AM LIGHTING THE PATH I HAVE LAID OUT BEFORE YOU. I AM SETTING THE CAPTIVES FREE AND SUPERCHARGING THE ATMOSPHERE. CAN YOU FEEL IT, MY CHILDREN? CAN YOU FEEL MY ANOINTING ALL AROUND YOU? CAN YOU FEEL ME SHIFTING AND MOVING AND CHANGING AND IGNITING THE ATMOSPHERE. DO YOU WANT TO SEE MY GLORY CLOUD RESTING IN THIS PLACE? EVEN NOW, MY ANGEL ARMIES ARE USHERING IN MY GLORY. JOIN THEM, MY SAINTS. LET HEAVEN AND EARTH JOIN TOGETHER IN MIGHTY WORSHIP AND INTERCESSION TO ELECTRIFY THIS REALM WITH MY ANOINTING. TO USHER IN SIGNS AND WONDERS AND MIRACLES THAT HAVE NOT BEEN EXPERIENCED IN A LONG TIME. THE TIME IS NOW! THE TIME IS NOW! THE TIME IS NOW!! SO, OPEN YOUR MOUTH AND CRY OUT! OPEN YOUR EARS AND LISTEN FOR MY VOICE! OPEN YOUR EYES AND SEE ME MOVING! SURRENDER, SURRENDER, SURRENDER ALL TO ME. HOLD NOTHING BACK! GIVE ME YOUR ALL AND WATCH ME MOVE!!

DO NOT LET THIS MOMENT PASS YOU BY, MY CHILDREN. I AM CALLING YOU TO REPENTANCE AND SURRENDER LIKE YOU HAVE NEVER FELT BEFORE. I AM CALLING YOU TO FALL DOWN ON YOUR KNEES AND CRY OUT. LET ME DO A MIGHTY WORK IN THIS PLACE AND LET IT START WITH YOU! IF MY PEOPLE WHO ARE CALLED BY MY NAME WILL HUMBLE THEMSELVES AND PRAY AND SEEK MY FACE AND TURN FROM THEIR WICKED WAYS. YOU HAVE HEARD THIS IN MY WORD, MY CHILDREN. YOU HAVE HEARD IT AND READ IT MANY, MANY TIMES. NOW, I AM ASKING YOU TO LET IT SOAK IN AND CHANGE YOU. HEALING STARTS HERE, HEALING STARTS NOW, HEALING STARTS WITH YOU! I AM LOOKING AT YOU! I AM CRYING OUT TO YOU! I AM DRAWING YOU UNTO ME. SO RUN INTO MY ARMS, FALL AT MY FEET AND SURRENDER. SURRENDER. SURRENDER. DO NOT WAIT ANOTHER DAY. DO NOT WAIT ANOTHER HOUR. DO NOT WAIT ANOTHER MINUTE. RUN!! RUN, MY DAUGHTER. RUN, MY SON. I AM STANDING HERE WITH OPEN ARMS. I WILL MEET YOU AT THE ALTAR. I WILL MEET YOU AT YOUR PLACE OF TOTAL SURRENDER. I AM HERE!!

A Word From Papa God To The Readers Of This Book

A WORD FROM PAPA GOD TO THE READERS OF THIS BOOK

OH, MY PRECIOUS DAUGHTER, MY CHOSEN SON, I LOVE YOU WITH AN EVERLASTING LOVE THAT KNOWS NO BOUNDS. I CHERISH YOU AND OUR TIME TOGETHER. I KNOW YOU ARE BUSY, BUT PLEASE DO NOT FORGET TO SPEND TIME WITH ME. I HAVE SO MUCH TO POUR INTO YOU. I HAVE SO MUCH TO TEACH YOU. I HAVE SO MUCH TO DO WITH YOU AND THROUGH YOU ON THIS EARTH. I AM YOUR BEST FRIEND, YOUR CONFIDANT, YOUR GREATEST LOVE, YOUR EVERYTHING. I AM ALWAYS HERE, I AM ALWAYS LISTENING, I AM ALWAYS READY TO LOVE ON YOU AND MEET YOUR NEEDS, NO MATTER HOW BIG OR HOW SMALL. NOTHING IS IMPOSSIBLE WITH ME. NOTHING. I HAVE HEARD MY CHILDREN ASK, "WHY DID YOU ALLOW THAT TO HAPPEN? WHY DIDN'T YOU SHOW ME WHERE TO GO AND WHAT TO DO?" I WANT TO, AND SOMETIMES I STEP IN AND JUST TAKE CARE OF IT. HOWEVER, YOU AND I ARE IN A RELATIONSHIP. I HAVE CREATED YOU WITH FREE WILL. YOU CAN MAKE YOUR OWN CHOICES. I WANT TO WALK WITH YOU EVERY STEP OF THE WAY. INVITE ME IN, MY CHILD, INVITE ME IN. LET ME WALK ONE STEP AT A TIME WITH YOU ON MY PERFECT PATH THAT I CREATED JUST FOR YOU. LET ME SHOW YOU ALL OF THE GREAT AND MIGHTY THINGS THAT WE CAN DO TOGETHER. YOU ARE SO IMPORTANT TO ME. YOU ARE MY BEAUTIFUL CREATION. TRUST

ME. I PROMISE THAT YOU CAN TRUST ME. I WILL NEVER LEAVE YOU OR FORSAKE YOU. I AM YOUR CONSTANT COMPANION. I COVER YOU WITH MY WINGS AND PROTECT YOU. STAY UNDER MY WINGS AND LET ME KEEP YOU SAFE FROM HARM. I LONG TO KEEP YOU SAFE FROM HARM. I AM GIVING YOU PEACE, JOY, LOVE, AND PROVISION. I LOVE TO GIVE MY CHILDREN GOOD GIFTS!

LOVE ALWAYS,

YOUR PAPA GOD
YOUR REDEEMER
YOUR RESCUER

1 Corinthians 13:4-13 TPT

Love is large and incredibly patient. Love is gentle and consistently kind to all. It refuses to be jealous when blessing comes to someone else. Love does not brag about one's achievements nor inflate its own importance. Love does not traffic in shame and disrespect, nor selfishly seek its own honor. Love is not easily irritated or quick to take offense. Love joyfully celebrates honesty and finds no delight in what is wrong. Love is a safe place of shelter, for it never stops believing the best for others. Love never takes failure as defeat, for it never gives up. Love never stops loving. It extends beyond the gift of prophecy, which eventually fades away. It is more enduring than tongues, which will one day fall silent. Love remains long after words of knowledge are forgotten. Our present knowledge and our prophecies are but partial, but when love's perfection arrives, the partial will fade away. When I was a child, I spoke about childish matters, for I saw things like a child and reasoned like a child. But the day came when I matured, and I set aside my childish ways. For now we see but a faint reflection of riddles and mysteries as though reflected in a mirror, but one day we will see face-to-face. My understanding is incomplete now, but one day I will understand everything, just as everything about me has been fully understood. Until then, there are three things that remain: faith, hope, and love—yet love surpasses them all. So above all else, let love be the beautiful prize for which you run.

A Prayer of Salvation

IF YOU HAVE NEVER GIVEN YOUR LIFE TO THE LORD THEN SIMPLY SAY THIS OUT LOUD:

FATHER, I AM CHOOSING TO SURRENDER ALL TO YOU, AND I ASK YOU TO COME INTO MY LIFE. I WANT TO LIVE THE REST OF MY LIFE WITH YOU AS MY LORD AND SAVIOR. SHOW ME HOW TO LIVE A LIFE THAT IS PLEASING TO YOU. I WANT PEACE, JOY, AND LOVE TO SURROUND ME. PLEASE FORGIVE ME OF MY SINS AND MAKE ME NEW AGAIN. IN JESUS NAME, AMEN.

JOHN 3:16-17 TPT
FOR HERE IS THE WAY GOD LOVED THE WORLD—HE GAVE HIS ONLY, UNIQUE SON AS A GIFT. SO NOW EVERYONE WHO BELIEVES IN HIM WILL NEVER PERISH BUT EXPERIENCE EVERLASTING LIFE. "GOD DID NOT SEND HIS SON INTO THE WORLD TO JUDGE AND CONDEMN THE WORLD, BUT TO BE ITS SAVIOR AND RESCUE IT!